# POLLUTION and CONSERVATION

## DAVID LAMBERT

# Topics

Some of the words in this book are printed in **bold**. Their meanings are explained in the glossary on page 30.

First published in 1985 by
Wayland (Publishers) Ltd
61 Western Road, Hove,
East Sussex BN3 1JD, England

© Copyright 1985 Wayland (Publishers) Ltd
3$^{rd}$ impression

Phototypeset by
Kalligraphics Ltd, Redhill, Surrey
Printed in Italy by
G. Canale & C.S.p.A., Turin
Bound in the UK by
The Bath Press, Avon

British Library Cataloguing in Publication Data:
Lambert, David
    Pollution and conservation. – (Topics)
    1. Pollution
    I. Title    II. Series
    363.7′3          TD174

ISBN 0–85078–593–6

# Contents

# Water at Risk

Our world teems with people: four thousand million of us. We need huge amounts of food and minerals, and we produce huge amounts of waste substances. This means we tend to **pollute** water, air, soil and living things, or spoil them by using them too much.

Scientists can often prevent, or mend, damage to the world around us. This protective work is **conservation**. Our book shows how pollution and overuse harm the world, and how conservation helps to save it.

*Metal-smelting has polluted this Peruvian river.*

*This river in Columbia is polluted by detergent.*

One of our most precious substances is water. Without fresh drinking water, we would die in a few days. But the water must be free from harmful impurities. Unfortunately, some water is not safe to drink, because it has been polluted by waste substances.

Body waste, or **sewage**, contains germs that cause diseases which may kill. These are common in poor countries, where sewage finds its way into wells or

*This is the only well in this African village.*

rivers, from which people get drinking water. In India, three young children die each minute from diarrhoea, caught from drinking polluted water.

One way to make sure water is pure is to pump it up from deep down in the ground. Germs cannot soak down through soil, sand and gravel to underground water.

Polluted water can be purified at a **water treatment works**. Gravel beds are used to help clean the water. This allows many city dwellers to safely drink water that has been used, and re-used, several times. Sadly, though, poor countries often cannot

*A water treatment works.*

afford to build expensive water treatment works.

Sewage can be treated, to make it less dangerous, at a sewage farm. Here, it is exposed to air in special tanks. But even treated sewage can cause trouble for animals that live in water, when it is pumped back

*Warning notices on a polluted beach in the USA.*

to lakes and rivers. In the USA, treated sewage killed millions of fish living in Lake Erie. The sewage contained chemicals, which formed food for tiny floating plants called algae. These multiplied in billions. Then they died and decayed – a process which used oxygen from the surrounding water. Without oxygen to breathe, many fish suffocated. But when engineers stopped adding sewage to the lake, the number of fish increased again.

**Insecticides**, **herbicides** and **fertilizers** are other dangers. Rainwater washes these off the land into rivers, lakes and seas, where they may kill water plants and animals. From factories and ships come other poisons such as chemicals, metal and **radioactive wastes**, and spilt oil. In the 1950s, one factory poured huge amounts of mercury waste into Minamata Bay, Japan. The mercury collected in fish and shellfish. Dozens of people who ate the fish became very ill, and some died.

*Notice the colour of the water in this polluted stream in St. Helens, Lancashire.*

*Oil from a wrecked tanker is cleared from a beach.*

Sometimes, a big oil tanker spills a huge load of sticky oil into the sea. The oil clogs seabirds' feathers and chokes them when they try to clean themselves. But oil companies now have ways to clean up oil floating on the sea, before it smothers beaches.

# Air at Risk

We cannot see the air we breathe. If air contains impurities, it is harmful.

Some of the worst air pollutants are gases and particles produced by burning certain fuels. Some fuels give off a lot of sulphur dioxide, a gas which mixes with fog to make dirty, yellow **smog**. Smog is unpleasant to breathe. It can even kill people. One winter, four thousand Londoners died from breathing smog. But since the 1950s, London's air has been much cleaner. The city simply stopped people burning fuels that gave off too much sulphur.

*Air pollution from a factory in Canada.*

*A haze of smog, caused by vehicle exhausts, covers the American city of San Francisco.*

In the USA, warm, sunny Los Angeles had a different problem. On bright days, a yellow-brown haze often darkened the sky and stung people's eyes. Scientists found that this was smog which formed when sunlight shone on exhaust gases from cars and trucks. Inventors designed special filters for vehicle exhausts, which helped to stop nitrogen oxide gas escaping. After that, the air became much cleaner.

Vehicle engines can give off other poisons. The most dangerous of all is lead, which is contained in petrol. Young children who breathe in lead particles could suffer brain damage. To prevent this, governments have started making petrol companies put less lead in petrol. A small amount of lead helps engines to work smoothly.

Some power stations and factories have very tall chimneys, so that harmful fumes escape high up – where wind carries them away. This keeps the air

*These signs in Tokyo, Japan, show how much pollution is in the air.*

clean in nearby cities. But the fumes still cause damage, by turning raindrops acidic. **Acid rain** rots stone buildings and steel railway lines. It has killed trees in German forests, and fish in parts of Sweden, Canada, and the USA.

*Fumes escape from a power station's tall chimneys.*

Many scientists think acid rain can be prevented by trapping harmful particles before they leave the chimneys. That means fitting expensive filters. In West Germany, people believe the cost is worthwhile. Meanwhile, people try adding lime (a white powder) to soil and water, to get rid of acid.

Other chemicals may harm the air in ways we do not fully understand. These include chemicals in certain fertilizers, spray cans, and the exhaust gases from supersonic planes. All might damage the invisible layer of **ozone** gas, high in the Earth's atmosphere. Ozone protects us from the Sun's strong, harmful ultraviolet rays. Without ozone, these rays could cause serious diseases in people, plants and animals. Some governments have begun to control the use of certain chemicals, in order to

*Spraying crops releases insecticide into the air.*

*Making use of the Sun's energy with solar panels in Tel Aviv, Israel.*

protect ozone.

We could save air from most pollutants if we stopped burning wood, coal, oil and gas. Instead, the electricity we need could be produced from the energy in wind, waves and sunshine. So far these provide only a tiny fraction of the energy we need.

# Soil at Risk

Soil is like a skin covering the surface of the land. Ingredients in soil nourish plants. Plants form food for creatures. So, without soil, there would be no crops or farm animals for us to eat. This makes soil a valuable substance, yet in many countries, people poison or remove much of it.

Sometimes, just trying to improve the soil harms it. This happens where engineers **irrigate** (water) hot, dry farmland that is not well drained. Water soaks into the soil. The Sun's heat sucks up the water. As the water rises, it brings up salts from deep

*A wasteland caused by cyanide pollution in Canada.*

down in the ground. So much salt collects near the surface of the soil that growing crops are poisoned. Good drainage could often solve this problem.

Wastes and rubbish dumped by factories, nuclear power plants and cities also damage soil. The wastes collect in the soil and get taken up by grass roots. If animals eat the grass, they may become ill and die.

*Sellafield nuclear waste processing plant, England.*

In some places, people accidentally destroy soil altogether. This risk is worst in hot, rainy countries, where many forests are chopped down. Tree roots hold soil particles together: without them rain washes the soil away. Then nothing grows.

*This Indonesian forest has been destroyed by chopping down trees for timber.*

Farmers can help to stop soil **erosion** by shaping the hillsides into giant steps, called terraces, which trap rainwater. Replanting forests with young trees, to replace those that have been chopped down, also helps to stop soil from being stripped away.

Hot, dry lands suffer soil erosion, too. When farmers plough dry soils, or herdsmen graze too many cattle, grass roots are killed. Wind blows the loosened, dusty soil away.

People *can* protect dry lands from damage. One way is to plant trees and grasses. Another way is to fence off **overgrazed** land, to keep out cattle or sheep until the grass grows well again. But in poor countries, where there are many hungry people, it

*Terracing helps prevent soil erosion.*

*A huge opencast copper mine in Australia.*

is difficult to protect soil. All soil has to be used to
try to cultivate food, even the poorer land, which is
most at risk from soil erosion.

Overusing soil by accident is damaging enough.
But some miners deliberately strip soil away, to get
at useful rocks beneath. **Opencast mining** of coal and
iron has cleared much soil from parts of the USA.

*Stacked crushed cars cover useful land in the USA.*

Covering up soil can be as bad as stripping it away. Heaps of waste **shale** from mines and **slag** from metalworks smother large areas of soil. In the USA, rubbish tips cover as much land as the whole state of Rhode Island.

There are ways to help save soil. Farmers can add fertilizer, to put back plant foods taken from the ground by last year's crops. That helps prevent erosion. But in poor countries, many farmers cannot afford fertilizer.

When an opencast mine is used up, earth-moving machines can cover the area with soil again. Conservation workers can plant trees on shale and slag heaps. Waste glass and paper can be re-used instead of dumped. City rubbish can be buried.

*Conservation workers clear a ditch.*

# Wildlife at Risk

People kill huge numbers of wild animals and plants, by plan or chance. Whole **species** have disappeared. Some others will not last long. A million species could become extinct by next century – unless the world acts fast to save them.

Farmers use insecticides to kill most insect pests. But sometimes, harmless animals then eat the pests and are poisoned.

Hunters shoot and trap big wild beasts, either for fun, food, or because the animals seem dangerous. A few years ago, nearly all India's tigers were wiped

*Tigers nearly became extinct in India.*

out. Few white and Javan rhinoceroses survive.
Whales and certain fish have grown scarcer.

Collectors can be a threat to wild animals and
plants. Hunters kill mother apes to catch their

*Armed rangers protect white rhinoceroses in Kenya.*

babies, which are sold as pets. Unusual plants, such as the Venus flytrap and stinking corpse lily, are uprooted. So, animals and plants grow scarce in the wild. Meanwhile, those taken and kept in poor conditions will not breed.

Most species disappear because they lose their habitats, or homes. Everywhere people clear forests, drain swamps and fill in ponds to make room for farming or building.

Conservationists work hard to save the world's

*A Venus flytrap, with a wasp trapped in its leaves.*

*Implanting embryos into mothers of a different breed could help save rare breeds. Here is an eland mother with her bongo calf.*

wildlife. Some scientists try using germs instead of insecticides to kill pests. The germs do not harm other animals. Governments pass laws to stop hunters and fishermen killing threatened species. Most nations no longer hunt rare whales. Many zoos do not buy from collectors; they breed their own rare animals and free some in the wild. Plant-research stations grow thousands of wild strains of wheat and rice, which may be used to breed from.

Best of all, nations set aside areas of forest, marsh, desert and coast as national parks or nature reserves. Wild animals live and multiply in safety there. The number of tigers is increasing fast in forests set aside for them in India.

All of us with gardens can help to save wild animals and plants, by making ponds and letting wild plants flourish in a corner of the garden. These make homes for frogs and butterflies.

But even protected wildlife may not be safe. In Africa, herdsmen and poachers invade national parks and damage plants and animals. Wardens try hard to keep them out. Conservation can be difficult and costly. But it is well worthwhile.

*A wild animal park in San Diego, USA.*

*A Kenyan national park warden and baby leopard.*

# Glossary

**Acid rain** Rain made acid by particles in air. The particles come from power stations, factory chimneys and vehicle exhausts.

**Conservation** Protecting something from pollution or other damage. Conservation can help to protect air, soil, water and wildlife.

**Erosion** Wearing away. Overusing soil can quickly cause it to be eroded.

**Fertilizer** A food which is added to soil to make plants grow better. Fertilizers include dead plants, animal waste, and chemicals, such as nitrates.

**Herbicides** Poisons that kill plants. Farmers spray herbicides on fields to kill weeds.

**Insecticides** Poisons that kill insects. Farmers spray insecticides on fields to kill insects that eat crops.

**Irrigation** Watering crops. The water comes from rivers, canals or wells. Ditches or sprinklers spread the water over fields.

**Opencast mining** Mining rock which is laid bare by scraping off the soil above.

**Overgrazing** When animals have eaten so much grass that the soil loses its nourishment, and is easily eroded.

**Ozone** A special kind of oxygen. Ozone forms a layer high in the atmosphere.

**Pollution** When water, air etc. are made impure by harmful or poisonous substances. A **pollutant** is a substance that causes pollution.

**Radioactive wastes** Wastes that give off harmful rays or particles. These come from substances used to produce nuclear energy.

**Sewage** Body waste carried off in water through pipes called sewers. Sewage farms treat sewage to make it non-poisonous. It may then be used as fertilizer.

**Shale** Flaky stone, often dug up with coal and left in heaps as waste.

**Slag** Stony waste produced in making iron or steel.

**Smog** A mixture of smoke and fog. Photochemical smog forms when sunlight acts on nitrogen oxide gas from vehicle exhausts.

**Species** A group of animals (such as dogs) or plants (such as potatoes). Members of one species can breed with each other, but usually not with members of another species.

**Strain** A group of plants or animals within a species.

**Water treatment works** Gravel beds and sprinkler systems that help to clean polluted water.

# Books to Read

*Conservation* by Michael Crawford (Danbury Press, 1976)

*Ecology 2000* edited by Sir Edmund Hillary (Michael Joseph, 1984)

*How to Save the World* by Robert Allen (Kogan Page, 1980)

*Pesticides and Pollution* by Kenneth Mellanby (Collins, 1967)

*Pollution* by Ian Breach (Danbury Press, 1975)

*Saving the Animals* by Bernard Stonehouse (Weidenfeld and Nicolson, 1981)

*Silent Spring* by Rachel Carson (Houghton Mifflin, 1962)

## Picture Acknowledgements

Geoffrey Berry 18; Camerapix Hutchison/Bernard Régent 12; Bruce Coleman/ Jane Burton 26, Norman Myers 19; Earthscan/German Castro 5; Robert Estall 16, 17, 22; Institute of Hydrology 6, 15; Institute of Terrestrial Ecology 9; Frank Lane/Ron Austing 27, Steve McCutcheon 8, R. Van Nostrand 28; Natural Science Photos/H. Frawley 23, M. Freeman 14, P.H. and S.L. Ward 25; Philippine Tourist Office/Adrian Dennis 20; Picturepoint *front cover*, 4, 8, 10, 13, 21; Southern Water Authority 7; Wayland Picture Library 29; World Wildlife Fund/P. Jackson 24.

# Index